KILBURN AND ITS

Dedicated to all those whose efforts have — or will — keep the Kilburn White Horse well groomed for the enjoyment of country lovers.

Kilburn and its Horse has been written by JOHN THORPE, Diary Editor of the Yorkshire Evening Post and an honorary member of the Kilburn White Horse Association, from material gathered by farmer FRED BANKS, of Wakendale House, Oldstead Grange — a long-time member, and a former chairman, of the Kilburn White Horse Association.

Sponsored by

ISBN 0 9525595 0 1

© First published April, 1995.

All rights reserved. No part of this book may be reproduced or transmitted in any form or by any means — electronic or mechanical, including photo-copying, recording or by any information storage and retrieval system — without the permission of the Publisher in writing.

Published by the Kilburn White Horse Association, Kilburn, North Riding of Yorkshire.

Printed by Simba Print Ltd, 8 Brandon Street, Armley Road, Leeds LS12 2EB.

Front and back cover photographs by **Edwin "Bill" Smith** of Woodman's Cottage, Kilburn.

FOREWORD
By James Herriot

WHEN I qualified as a veterinary surgeon more than 55 years ago, our profession was in the doldrums and jobs were scarce. The only position I could find was in Yorkshire and since I had grown up in the big city of Glasgow I wondered what sort of place I was coming to.

Like most people from Scotland I knew nothing about Yorkshire and, in fact, was under the impression that there was no scenic beauty outside Scotland.

The Lake District, Devon and Cornwall and the like were familiar, but Yorkshire had no such romantic ring and I was prepared for an uninteresting countryside.

Yorkshire Dales

My first view of the Yorkshire Dales dispelled this delusion. I immediately fell in love with them but our practice headquarters were in Thirsk, a long way from there, and I was prepared to be disappointed.

My fears, however, were groundless. I had only spent a few days in Thirsk when I was called to the village of Kilburn

James Herriot holding Bodie, his favourite Border Terrier.

3

which was only one of the enchanting hamlets scattered along the slopes of the Hambleton Hills.

As I approached the village I had one of my most delightful surprises — my first sight of the White Horse of Kilburn. This is a most magnificent enterprise; the huge white figure of a horse cut from the face of Roulston Scar, a cliff overhanging the village.

I find it difficult to describe the thrill I felt at the time, and it is something which has remained with me over the years.

Distance

Even from many miles distance I know when I am approaching my own part of the world. The White Horse is there, apparently marching alongside from its lofty position in the hills overlooking the Plain of York.

As a young man it was one of my favourite outings to take my small children to sit up there on the moorland grass and savour what must be one of the finest panoramic views in England; 50 miles of chequered fields stretching away to the long bulk of the Pennines.

Helpers

These outings continued with my grandchildren, and there seemed to be no end to their delight in climbing up the long row of steps and wandering in the crystal fresh air along the hillside path to the top of Sutton Bank.

I naturally could not wait to find out about the origin of this wonder and it turned out that the horse was cut from the hillside in 1857 by the village schoolmaster and 30 helpers and kept white by whitewash and chalk chippings.

Over the years it has been a constant task, and worry, to keep it white and I found this booklet, **Kilburn and its Horse**, contained a wealth of information about the long struggle against nature, and sometimes vandalism.

Heart-Breaking

The booklet deals with this, sometimes in a gently humorous way, but it must have been a heart-breaking chore for the dedicated few who continued their efforts against the odds.

Along with many thousands of others, I am grateful for their efforts because, despite my admission that I am biased, I am certain that they have perpetuated one of the finest and most exciting landmarks in the countryside of England.

James Herriot

James Herriot, the pseudonym of author Alf Wight, died on Thursday February 23, 1995. He was 78. This foreword to Kilburn and its Horse was submitted by him on Tuesday February 21, 1995, and was his last written work.

White horses, and all that...

THIS is the story of a white horse. Not any white horse, but the one that's "stabled" high above the picture-postcard village of Kilburn in the North Riding of Yorkshire.

It's not the only white horse in the United Kingdom — eleven white horses are still visible and a further four are known to have existed but have, through neglect, disappeared.

The most famous carved horse is the one at Uffington, in Berkshire — Tykes would disagree and say it's the Kilburn figure that's ahead of the field.

Animal

The Uffington animal is, though, thought to be the oldest. Its existence is recorded in the 13th Century.

Cutting hill figures seems to have become a popular pastime in the 18th and 19th centuries, although the one at Pewsey, in Wiltshire, was "born" as recently as 1937. It replaced an older version which had disappeared.

But this is the history and background to the Kilburn White Horse — the largest of all Britain's White Horses in surface area covering just over an acre. That's the way its designers wanted it — the biggest White Horse in the land.

The Kilburn White Horse was carved on Roulston Scar in the 1850s. It was an idea of Thomas Taylor, a native of Kilburn, who'd left his home to join the thriving provisions business of his brother, William, in London.

During his sojourn there he came across some white horses cut in the hills in Berkshire.

One of the friends whom he had left in Kilburn was John Hodgson, the village schoolmaster who also practised as a land surveyor.

Believing that John Hodgson would be enthusiastic about the idea of having a similar horse in the North, Taylor wrote to him about it and suggested that Roulston Scar would be a suitable site and enclosed a drawing of his idea.

Cliffside

John Hodgson did take up the scheme with great enthusiasm and set about surveying the cliffside, using his pupils to help plot it out.

To determine the outline, Hodgson drove 'stobs' (stakes) into the ground and, on completion of this part of the work, volunteers from the village cut away the scrub and exposed the rock. The Horse came to light in November, 1857.

The Making of the Horse

There's a first hand description of the making of the Kilburn White Horse from Thomas Goodrick - a pupil at the village school - who helped remove the turves when the figure was cut.

Thomas lived in the village all his life and worked as a cobbler. He was a Methodist local preacher whose hobby was writing verse. He died in 1929.

This is how he recorded the making of the horse.

In a little village school, when the master had gone out,
The children were delighted to romp about and shout;
But soon John Hodgson came, with a letter in his hand,
And a drawing of a horse, which he had closely scanned,
It came from Thomas Taylor who in London did reside;
Saying can you please make a horse on Roulston Scar hillside?

I've just come back from Berkshire, and a pretty sight I've seen;
A big horse on the hillside, with coat so white and clean.
I thought of bonny Kilburn, a place so dear to me,
A white horse on the hillside, a nice landmark would be.
So he took his scale and compass, saying "I'll do my best to try,
To make a horse quite big enough my friend to satisfy."

When the plan was finished, and everything complete,
He looked around the scholars sitting on the seat,
And called out John Rowley, the biggest of the lot,
Saying, "Please can you help me to measure out the plot?"
The work was very hard, but with great skill and care
The master and the boy, both tried to do their share.

They put in little stobs and left them fair in site,
To guide the men who cut the sods to do their work aright.
Then thirty one men of Kilburn, who knew how to use the spade
All went to work so heartily that soon the plot was bared.
Although the work was difficult, they managed it quite well,
And only one man lost his feet and rolled right down the hill.

*But when they found he was not hurt, it caused a lot of mirth
When an avalanche of sods came down and pinned him to the earth.
The school was closed that day but the boys instead of play,
Climbed up the hill to help the men to throw the sods away.
In November 1857 the white horse first was seen,
With a brand new coat of lime which made him white and clean.*

*A little girl, when passing by in great amazement said,:
"O Dad!, how will they stable him at night when he goes to bed?"
From Brafferton to Boroughbridge, Boston Spa and Wetherby,
From York, Knaresborough and Harrogate, the white horse you can see.
And scores of other places; and people in the train
When passing to and fro can see him very plain.*

*They come from near and far, to sit upon his eye,
And stand upon his back, on the hill so steep and high.
They gaze upon the landscape so beautiful and grand,
O'er the golden Vale of Mowbray one of the finest in the land.*

*And every year eight men do go, to cut the weeds off as they grow
For if he long neglected be, there would not be a horse to see.
And, when the lime is washed away instead of white he turns quite grey.
So now and then there comes a time when he needs a good thick coat of lime.*

The Early Years

A tranquil view from Thirsk Road, Kilburn

THE Kilburn White Horse has to be one of Yorkshire's best-known landmarks, visible as it is for many miles around.

In its early years, the horse was looked after with tender, loving care.

Jack Silson, who lived in Bradford, was a regular visitor for 70 years. He told a writer in the 1930s that he had visited the White Horse as a boy and young man from 1870.

Jack recalled that the figure was regularly weeded and whitened, and was kept in tip-top condition.

Fred Banks, who looked after the horse for 30 years and was stalwart chairman of the Kilburn White Horse Association until he handed over the reins to Debbie Bradley in 1993, has discovered one reason why.

Says Fred: "The Bolton family kept the Forresters Arms in Kilburn. Two family members — George and John — are listed on the original list of subscribers.

"The Boltons look to have collected donations from their patrons for the up-keep of the horse. The money they raised probably paid for the lime for whitening.

Farmers

"According to Mrs Goodrick, widow of Thomas who wrote the verses about the hill carving, local farmers sent horses and carts to take lime to the site, and farm hands spread it over the surface without charging for their labours.

"It's not clear how long this state of affairs continued, but it does seem that after the first 30 years — and many of those who helped carve the horse having passed away — the initial enthusiasm was waning.

"There were, according to Mrs Goodrick, special cleaning operations for Queen Victoria's Golden Jubilee, and later for the Coronation of King Edward VII.

"But it seems grooming became less regular after the turn of the century and that the responsibility was falling mainly on the shoulders of the Boltons of the Forresters Arms, and the Kirk family who were tenants of the land upon which the horse is carved."

Troubled Times

BY 1910, the Kilburn White Horse was in trouble. In that year a cloudburst over Kilburn, and the nearby village of Oldstead, hurled torrential rain on the terrain.

An old grey mare?

According to Sidney Maw of Kilburn, deep gullies were washed out in several places on the surface of the horse, and a quantity of rock was dislodged around the figure's shoulder. The line of the belly was also spoilt.

All this at a time when interest in the horse was at an all time low in the village. The Boltons and the Kirks still collected donations, but the money was used to pay men to hoe and whiten the figure. There were no volunteers to do the job.

By now all the money was hardly sufficient to maintain the figure, let along make improvements.

Rain and snow are still a nightmare by the way. Erosion does not occur to any great extent without there being large quantities of surface water.

But substantial damage can be caused by heavy rain and by the sudden melting of drifted snow.

They're used to snow around the Hambleton Hills, and even now those who care for the horse look skyward when showers are forecast.

For if snow comes on a North, or North East, wind it's swept over the edge of the escarpment and forms deep drifts on the horse. True, the horse is white but so is the rest of Roulston Scar.

If the thaw sets in and is accompanied by heavy rain, substantial damage is likely to the surface of the horse.

The Yorkshire Evening Post Gallops to the Rescue

As the horse really started to deteriorate after the ending of the First World War, visitors from the West Riding started voicing their concern to their local newspaper - the *Yorkshire Evening Post* - and the paper started highlighting readers' worries about the state of the horse.

As an opening shot in April, 1925, the *Yorkshire Evening Post* reprinted the verses penned by Thomas Goodrick with a request for subscriptions to a fund for the figure's restoration.

Like many subsequent appeals by the *Yorkshire Evening Post* the response from readers was immediate and the paper lost no time in pressing home the message. A film crew was even engaged to record the work on the horse.

In memory of the 1925 appeal.

"The film of the Kilburn White Horse being groomed should form an interesting feature of entertainment at the Scala Picture House, in Leeds, next week," wrote a *Yorkshire Evening Post* staff journalist on May 29, 1925.

Letters, and money poured in, and the fund soon accumulated £137 19s. Included in this sum was £1 to be contributed annually by the Church Commissioners - the owners of the land - and ten United States dollars from Mr Leonard Peckitt, of New York, who was born at Oldstead Hall and brought up at Carlton Husthwaite with the "old horse constantly in sight."

Bank

With the £137 19s from the *Yorkshire Evening Post* appeal in the bank, villagers decided to set up a three man team of trustees to administer the fund and put the white back in to the Kilburn White Horse.

The Rev H A K Hawkins, Vicar of Kilburn, was Trust chairman; George Bolton, a descendant of the Boltons who ran the Forresters Arms, was enlisted as was Robert Thompson, a young man who had just started furniture making as a career.

This three-man band set about organising the restoration of the figure.

One hundred pounds was invested in 5 per cent War Loan, and the £37 was spent on restoration.

Close Eye

The *Yorkshire Evening Post* continued to keep a close eye on the horse on Roulston Scar, and on May 29, 1925, the paper reported that grooming was in progress; weeds had been removed, and many tons of chalk had been bought from Wharram Chalk Pits, near Malton, and spread over the surface.

Although the paper's White Horse Fund had closed, donations kept rolling in.

A plaque recording the *Yorkshire Evening Post's* appeal in 1925 was erected, and still stands in the car park at the foot of the steps that lead to the horse.

Trust

The new-found funds of the Trust allowed weeding to be carried out yearly, and occasionally the surface was limed.

But after a decade there was trouble again. The interest on the War Loan had fallen from £5 a year to £3 10s. There wasn't enough money coming in to cover costs. By 1939, the Trust had a deficit of £6 5s 9d after £9 was spent on buying six tons of ground lime in 1937, and another £3 12s spent on weeding during 1938 and 1939.

The Wartime Horse

MONEY may have been tight, but the worst that had happened so far was the Kilburn White Horse had become an old grey mare.

It had, though, a worse fate in store. Soon after the outbreak of the Second World War, in 1939, military top brass in Whitehall were concerned about this landmark loved by so many from the West Riding.

The military strategists reasoned that the horse could be used as a landmark to guide enemy aircraft to the Allied bomber stations that were dotted around the Vale of Mowbray that stretched out below.

Camouflage

They ordered that the horse should be hidden from view with camouflage netting and turf.

Villagers were further ordered — on pain of death? — that the covering was not to be removed until after the ending of hostilities.

Some good — but not that much — did come out of the horse's "disappearance"...interest from the War Loan stock accumulated because it couldn't be spent by order of Winston Churchill's military advisers.

In 1946, under the guidance of Robert Thompson and George Bolton, weeding and whitening resumed. Lo and behold, the white horse was visible again, but it was still an uphill battle to prevent erosion.

Lightening, they say, doesn't strike twice in the same place. It did at Roulston Scar.

Towards the end of August, 1949, another freak cloudburst flooded Kilburn's village street to such a depth that people could not find the bridges that span the beck.

One local, thinking he knew exactly where the bridge was to his home, rode on merrily only to end up in the raging torrent.

Village

Bad it may have been in the village, but it was even worse high on Roulston Scar.

Water from the airfield at the top of Sutton Bank cascaded over the neck, and around the rocky outcrop on the shoulder of the horse.

A mass of rock was undermined by the torrent and fell down the hillside, settling below the front legs of the figure. That rock remains there today!

Such a massive landfall left a large area of exposed rock, and landslips remain a problem to this day.

The Rev John Bromley had been appointed the new vicar of Kilburn and he became chairman of the Trustees. George Bolton and Robert Thompson were still faithful servants of the horse, but the financial pressure was on again..they'd only a guaranteed income of £4 10s a year to spend on their favourite "animal".

Survived

That the horse survived during the years after the Second World War and until 1963 is largely due to Robert Thompson who, by this time, had established his mouse furniture business and must have had other things on his mind.

But Robert was a great supporter of the horse, and he sent his men from the workshops to weed and spread whitening material. Even his lorry was pressed in to service and used to transport the chalk and lime.

Robert's generosity during these lean years is still a source of great comfort to those who today look after the figure.

And the *Yorkshire Evening Post* continued to report happenings on Roulston Scar. The newspaper reported "Bob" Thompson's efforts.

He summed up his feelings in 1949, thus: "It takes four men a full day in Spring, and a full day in Summer, to hoe and weed the ground at a cost of £1 per man per day.

Transport

"And every third year the horse has to be relimed, or treated with Carbide. It costs £10 to transport 12 tons of Carbide from Long Marston; it costs £7 8s to cover the cost of labour applying it. To cover the figure completely would take 40 tons of Carbide.

"He's a fine weather 'oss — he turns dirty grey when wet.

"It makes me mad when people say we should paint it. Have you ever tried to paint a ploughed field?

"Spent Carbide is the best stuff, but we can't get any more."

13

Coronation Year

QUEEN Elizabeth II was preparing to take the Throne of England in 1953, but 200 miles away from London the people of Kilburn were again turning their attention to their white charger. It was not a pretty sight.

The Rev John Bromley again contacted the *Yorkshire Evening Post* with a plea for help. He estimated that £200 was needed to restore the surface. Ewart Clay was assistant editor at the time. He was very supportive, and again the paper launched an appeal.

Leslie Driffield

Legend

The paper's editor, Alan Woodward, was a friend of snooker legend Leslie Driffield. At the time Driffield was the world amateur billiard champion who, from his home in Moortown, Leeds, could see the white horse with the aid of binoculars.

Leslie offered to give a series of exhibition matches, the proceeds from which would go the the YEP fund. They were a great success, raising over £120 which — together with generous donations from *Yorkshire Evening Post* readers — again saved the horse, proving that Kilburn and its White Horse were still popular with the town and city dwellers of the West Riding.

But the horse didn't have its new coat by the time of the Coronation. It did though the following year.

The Forestry Commission — who'd leased most of the southern and western slopes of the Hambleton escarpment from the Church Commissioners two years earlier — also dug into its coffers and made a contribution to the horse's upkeep.

Death of Robert "Mouseman" Thompson

FAMED the world over for his oak furniture bearing a small mouse, Robert Thompson — who'd worked so hard to preserve the horse — passed away in 1955. It was yet another blow for the small band who still believed the hill carving had a future.

Says local farmer Fred Banks: "Robert understood more about the figure's preservation than anyone, and his efforts over a period of 30 years undoubtedly saved it from extinction.

"By now famous the world over for his mouse oak furniture, he was the little-known saviour of the much larger horse."

Grandson

Robert was succeeded by his grandson, Robert Cartwright, on the Trust. The love of the horse ran in the family, for Thompson's grandson began to organise some of the work on the figure which had not been done by the Forestry Commission.

Soon after Robert's death George Bolton, last of the trio who'd made up the trustees after the 1925 public appeal for cash, passed away. Bob Cartwright and the Rev Frank Peltor — who'd become vicar of Kilburn the year that Bob Thompson died — continued the drive to save the horse.

Mr Peltor left Kilburn in 1959 and again villagers were becoming concerned about the state of the horse on the hill.

Robert Thompson in his drawing office.

Another crisis, another committee

AFTER the departure of Frank Peltor, John Douglas was installed as Kilburn's vicar. He lost no time in meeting Robert Cartwright, with farmer Tom Banks and other local worthies. They believed the Forestry Commission should hand back responsibility for work on the horse to a committee of local people.

John Weston-Adamson, of Oldstead Hall, was elected chairman — the first non-cleric to head the White Horse supporters.

John proved to be an enthusiastic, energetic and imaginative chairman. In 1964 a new appeal for funds was launched; brochures were printed and distributed all over Yorkshire and the North. And the new committee proved itself.

Rev Douglas was well-practised in the art of fund-raising; the Cartwrights — Robert and John — had previously looked after the horse, a job they'd inherited from their grandfather, Robert Thompson; Paul Golding and Fred Suffield had previous experience working on the figure, and Tom Banks proved an able secretary.

Bob Cartwright

Tom Banks

West Riding

Again the people of the West Riding dug in to their pockets and provided cash, so did local landlords around the Thirsk area. Thirsk Amateur Dramatics, the Leeds Male Voice Choir, local Members of Parliament, schools and hundreds of private individuals helped swell the fund. By 1966 the fund to restore the horse stood at £2,179, of which £858 was spent on immediate remedial work.

John enlisted the services of MR R C Gibson — then surveyor for the North Riding County Council.

Gibson's findings were gloomy. The horse, he said, was in poor shape; needed extensive and immediate restoration and it was going to cost a lot of money to get it well groomed again.

Gibson, who was co-opted on to the committee as an advisor, refused payment for his services.

Things started to happen. County Council workmen, under Gibson's supervision, set about restoration and were paid by the White Horse Committee.

Caring

The County Council's involvement caring for the horse was continued by Lt Col Gerald Leech when he took over on Gibson's retirement.

By 1971, Robert Cartwright, committee treasurer, reported a balance in the fund of £4,210. It was agreed the appeal launched in 1964 should be closed.

It was thought, wrongly with hindsight, that £4,210 invested would be sufficient for the continued maintenance of the horse.

They hadn't reckoned with Corporation Tax which took 40 per cent of the interest on the capital.

If only they could get this tax burden lifted. They did. In 1972 the Charity Commission was asked to grant the White Horse Restoration Fund charitable status, thus exempting it from tax.

After protracted negotiations carried out by the late Theo Nicholson, they got their wish, subject to certain conditions.

In 1973 the committee was dissolved and the Kilburn White Horse Association came into being. It satisfied the legal requirements of the Charity Commission, and is still in existence today.

Young Farmers Ride to the Rescue

YOUNG farmers — young by definition; some of them farmers and used to looking after the land — rode to the rescue of the White Horse when the contract with the council highways department for maintaining it was ended in 1977.

First on the scene with muscle power was the Helmsley Young Farmers' Club. Its members rolled up their sleeves and set about weeding, clearing scrub and re-turfing the outline of the figure before whitening the horse.

Once again it could be seen for miles around. Two of those Helmsley Young Farmers — John Bielby and Robert Wilson — still look kindly on the horse they helped revive and are valued members of the Kilburn White Horse Association.

Next it was the turn of the Thirsk Young Farmers' Club to offer a helping hand.

Frosts

During the winter of 1980/81, severe frosts, over long periods, broke up the surface of the horse around its hindquarters. It fell away leaving only bedrock and limestone brash. Another big maintenance job was needed.

The Association decided to terrace this area using wooden rails and iron pegs to keep the next application of chalk in place.

The Thirsk YFC were worth their weight in gold!

When the White Horse is groomed every three years or so, it's again the Young Farmers clubs that prepare for some real graft.

Donation

It's not a labour of love, though, they get a donation from the Association. Others to help over the years include staff of Middle Heads Outdoor Pursuit Centre at Pickering, pupils and staff of Beverley Grammar School, North York Moors National Park and scores of individuals.

Why don't you...?

FOR most of its life, the White Horse of Kilburn has been dogged by the elements and its "stable lads and lasses" strapped for cash to keep it well groomed.

The keepers of the horse have never been short of "helpful" advice. Most of the improvements and repairs have been the result of someone's ideas. They are the suggestions that worked.

But what about the ones that didn't?

Farmer Fred Banks, who's been involved in caring for the horse for three decades — just like his father before him — recalls a few.

Nature

"Why don't you just forget about the horse, it's more bother than it's worth."

That the horse be abandoned, and nature left to take its course, was only suggested by a minority and, fortunately, an idea disregarded by all right-thinking Yorkshiremen and women.

"Paint it?"

This, says Fred, is an idea frequently put forward. Robert "Mouseman" Thompson, in his own blunt way, had a quick answer to this question. Bob used to retort: "Have YOU ever tried to paint a ploughed field?" He never found anyone who had!

But such a suggestion, despite the enormity of the task, has been at the back of many people's minds.

In fact, in 1962, Robert Cartwright, Thompson's grandson who'd taken over as treasurer and Custodian of the horse, sought advice on the best materials to apply.

He wanted to get away from using powdered lime which washed away with the first rain storm. Robert wrote to both ICI and Earles Cement. Both companies agreed what should be used.

In a note to Robert, they wrote: "Place one bushel of good fresh lime in a barrel with 20lbs of beef tallow; slake with hot water and cover with a sackcloth to keep in the steam. When the lime is slaked, the tallow will have disappeared having formed a chemical compound with lime."

Sound Stuff

This, says Fred, sounds just the stuff, but how does one mix sufficient to cover more than an acre, transport it to the hillside, and then apply it?

"This may not have been the first time such a mixture had been suggested," says Fred who farms at Oldstead.

"As a schoolboy in the early 1930s, I remember a strange white mixture being stirred in a barrel behind the Forresters Arms by landlord George Bolton (supervising), and Harry "Gunner" Raine (mixing).

"Gunner, so named because of his oft recounted exploits in the Artillery in the First World War, was not enthusiastic about the mixture.

Recipe

"He said it stuck to everything, and it 'weant' come off. We don't know if 'Gunner' stuck to the recipe but it certainly stuck to him. For the next few days, whenever he passed the school, he was followed by jeering children shouting 'piebald 'oss, 'piebald 'oss'. I heard nothing more about this mixture."

Fred Banks

Concrete it?

THIS is another idea which has frequently been put forward. Several times feasibility studies have been done. Experts reckon that if the concrete was applied to the existing surface, it would be unnatural and not aesthetically acceptable — certainly not in today's 'green' world.

Says Fred Banks: "It could, of course, be coated with chalk chips while still wet and the surface would be restored — a sort of pebble dashing.

"But Roulston Scar is so unstable, it would be difficult to fix several hundred tons of concrete horse on a hillside that's almost vertical. You could end up with two horses — the original one, and a pebble-dashed one in the car park below.

Rock

"If the horse had been on a gentle slope of, say, 1 in 20 - and the underlying rock been secure - concrete could have been a permanent solution.

"But lichens do grow on a concrete surface leading to discoloration, so the horse would still have to be whitened regularly."

Spray the horse with plastic?

THIS was an idea that came from a firm specialising in sprayed on coatings for roofs and walls. The plastic material used is totally impervious; can be white, and because the surface is so smooth, mosses and lichens would be kept at bay.

"It was a costly solution, but we believed the American company would supply the material at very low cost as an advertising ploy," recalls Fred.

United States

"An inspection of the horse was made by a representative of the US firm but he decided the scheme had too many pitfalls.

"In fact, the same drawbacks that would have existed had a concrete surface been laid.

"There were also worries about plastic being acceptable in such a stunning environment, and it was feared there was again a danger of ending up with two horses. This was another idea which became a non-starter."

Use a plastic woven net to hold the surface material?

THIS is a product which is used to stabilise roads in wet and swampy areas. The makers did send a representative to look at the horse, but he couldn't recommend using such a net. It was felt by experts that a net could not hold such a vast weight of chalk chips on a near vertical surface; sunlight would degrade it, and it could not be guaranteed to last very long.

Looking grey

BRAIN power has been applied over the years trying to find a permanent solution to stop the White Horse looking like a grey mare.

But just showering it with fresh chalk chips whenever it begins to look slightly off colour would result in a massive accumulation of chalk. This would be difficult to hold in place on the steep slope.

That's what made paint look an attractive alternative. And, in 1992, the Kilburn White Horse Association was offered a free supply by a company specialising in marker paints for sports fields.

Paint

The firm, Fleet Markers Ltd, delivered the paint in bulk and loaned napsack sprayers.

It was not an easy task painting the horse, but the first results were excellent and local people said they'd never seen the horse look better groomed.

But the whiteness proved to be short-lived. By the Autumn of 1993 the surface had resumed its dark grey look when wet, and off-white when dry. A combination of circumstances seemed to have worked against the painting idea.

Chalk

First, the unstable chalk chips only got painted on one side and were liable to turn over through the actions of melting snow, thunderstorms and the patter of human feet.

It also appeared there was a chemical reaction between the paint, the chalk and the atmosphere which diminished the whitening effect that locals had so admired when the paint was first applied.

During the winter months mosses and lichens grow on chalk and while they die off in hot weather, the surface never regains its whiteness. While fungicide added to the paint seemed to delay the lichen growth, it did not prevent it.

Having had the painting experience, the Kilburn White Horse Association is reluctant to commit money, which is in short supply, to hire equipment and buy more paint without being certain it would be more successful than the last attempt.

A mouse for the horse!

TOM Banks, father of Fred, couldn't believe his ears when he sought some cash from the English Tourist Board back in the 1970s.

Tom was secretary of the Kilburn White Horse Association and was always on the look-out for new sources of income to keep the figure well groomed.

A man from the tourist board decided to travel to Kilburn to see the horse for himself.

He showed very little interest in the horse, saying that since it was already in existence it would attract tourists whatever its condition.

What was needed, said the man from the tourist board, was a companion for the horse.

Furniture

And since Kilburn was the village where Robert Thompson's craftsmen were busily engaged on making "mouse" furniture, a white mouse carved alongside the White Horse would be an appropriate additional attraction.

The tourist board, he said, would look favourably on making a contribution towards the carving of the white mouse.

But the idea went down like a lead balloon with those charged with protecting the White Horse.

Creature

They were already landed with one figure to preserve and restore, and the thought of another creature — no matter how small — was just too much to contemplate.

The Association decided discretion was the better part of valour. They decided to forgo English Tourist Board money.. and confined the idea of a mouse to the dustbin of history.

Thompson's cottage and outbuilding workshops in the 1920s.

Kilburn today

Towards the Millenium

YORKSHIRE Evening Post Editor Chris Bye and some friends were walking the Hambleton Hills when they came across the stone at the foot of the steps leading to the White Horse which commemorates the paper's involvement in raising funds to restore the hill figure back in 1925.

The stone, like the horse, had seen better days. It was weather-worn and covered in moss.

Returning to the YEP offices in Wellington Street, Leeds, Bye called in John Thorpe — the paper's Diary Editor and someone who was born and raised in the North Riding, a dozen miles from Kilburn.

The Editor's instructions were clear. He wanted the stone cleaned, or a new one put in its place. After visiting the horse, and fortuitously bumping into farmer Fred Banks selling White Horse pins in the car park, Thorpe learned that funds were barely adequate to carry out another whitening.

On hearing this, Bye gave the go-ahead for Thorpe — through his Yorkshire Diary column in the *Yorkshire Evening Post* — to launch another White Horse appeal.

John Thorpe

Appeal Led by a Filly

DEBBIE Bradley is at peace in the great outdoors, riding out in the spectacular countryside around her Coxwold home.

She's never lived anywhere else but among the tranquility of the acres where the Vale of York butts up against the Hambleton Hills a handful of miles from the market town, and horse racing centre, of Thirsk.

Debbie is a nanny — "I don't like being called an au pair, it gives an impression of short skirts and frilly pinnies".

She's a young lady who oozes confidence, relaxes by riding horses and ponies, likes the odd half pint of beer and finds solace in music.

Debbie, 26, has, though, become the Horse Woman of Kilburn, by saddling up and taking on one of the country's toughest stable jobs — making sure Kilburn's White Horse is so well groomed it could win the "best turned out" prize in any race.

There's never been a younger chair of the White Horse Association — a registered charity that's a sort of Kilburn Jockey Club.

Debbie Bradley - painting the horse.

28

That doesn't worry Debbie, nor the other members of the Association.

She came under starter's orders on January 1st, 1994. She's been in great demand since, and has become a media celebrity.

Debbie, though, doesn't appear to be star-struck by the media spotlight; she's got her feet fixed on terra firma, and her eyes glued on her "baby" — the White Horse.

Volunteer

Why did she volunteer for the unpaid job that takes up hours of her time?

"Because it's part of my life," she says,"Wherever I've gone I've been able to see 'the horse'.

"When I went away for the day as a kid, I knew I was almost home when I could see it.

"I got involved with the White Horse around 1983 when I helped other young farmers spread chalk chippings over it every few years.

"I joined the Association in 1992, and when Fred Banks — then its chairman — said he wanted to step down, I let my name go forward. I'm still learning a lot from Fred who looked after the horse for 30 years".

High hopes

MARGARET Gomersall spends her days watching folk go up, up and away in gliders launched from the airfield on the top of Sutton Bank that's home to the Yorkshire Gliding Club where she's secretary.

But Margaret has got another love that's "tethered" on Roulston Scar at the end of the gliding club's runway — the White Horse.

She loves the beast so much that in 1991 she agreed to take over as treasurer of the Kilburn White Horse Association when octogenarian Bill Chambers decided it was time to relinquish the purse strings he'd controlled for two decades.

Margaret Gomersall

29

Just two years later Bill died.

Says Margaret: "Kilburn is where my heart is, and the White Horse is part of our heritage, just as much as places like Castle Howard and York Minster."

Margaret knows her unpaid job as treasurer will never be a walk-over unless, by some "miracle", tens of thousands of pounds suddenly race Kilburn's way.

Paul Golding

Keeping a record

PAUL Golding has lived in Kilburn since 1947, but he's known the village since he was 14 when he became an apprentice craftsman in Robert Thompson's "mouse" workshop.

Born in Wombleton, near Kirkbymoorside, and educated at Malton Grammar School, Paul used to travel to work every day on the train. He was called up to serve King and Country during the Second World War and spent four years in the Royal Air Force. He was aircrew and flew on numerous sorties over Europe.

Paul returned to his job making Thompson furniture after his demob. His speciality was crafting church work — pews, screens and the like for places of worship all over the country.

His work can be seen in Ampleforth College, and Ampleforth Abbey, but Paul also worked on numerous churches in Wales — including Bangor Cathedral.

Apprentice

Paul worked for Thompsons for 51 years, retiring when he was 65 in 1987.

It was in 1963, when the famous hill carving was probably in its worst condition and in danger of disappearing, that he first joined the Kilburn White Horse Association — the guardians of the horse.

He became Association secretary in 1974 — a position he's held for 21 years.

By Chris Bye, Editor, Yorkshire Evening Post.

IT is almost as if my life has been overseen by the White Horse of Kilburn. The reassuring image always seems to have been there. As a child I could see it on clear days from my bedroom window; in the right conditions it was even visible from my grammar school near Tadcaster.

Later in life I even had a house designed and built so I could see the reliable white image shining out across the Vale of York.

As a Yorkshire Post reporter I even flew over it, courtesy of an RAF Tornado squadron.

But for some reason over the years I never got walking in the Hambleton Hills to view the chalky equine icon at first hand; not, that is, until the summer of 1994.

Uncovered

It was then I uncovered another connection. There in the undergrowth at the foot of the steps taking walkers up to the airfield at the top of Sutton Bank was a moss-covered, and part weathered, stone bearing fading lettering. I could just make out the words *Yorkshire Evening Post*.

Closer examination revealed the legend: 'A restoration fund was subscribed by readers of the YEP and the residue of £100 was invested to provide for the triennial 'grooming' of the figure.'

Chris Bye

31

A mixed sense of pride and sadness swept over me. This was a connection which should be revitalised. This landmark's future must be secured and the connection with Yorkshire's biggest selling newspaper renewed.

Within weeks readers rallied round to help raise money for the horse's renovation; the newspaper itself paid for the old stone to be replaced with a new one.

After 70 years a happy relationship has been reborn....and the burning white image of the trusty old White Horse will be with me for the rest of my days.

Kilburn - The Village

OFTEN described as "nestling" beneath the Hambleton Hills which form the south-westerly bastion of the North York Moors, Kilburn is really split in two. Low Kilburn is 315ft above sea-level, and High Kilburn 418ft.

The village has a long history — traces of prehistoric man have been found in the district; half-way up Sutton Bank is a Bronze Age tomb circa 1400 B.C. The Romans knew the place, and Scandinavian invaders settled there in the 9th century.

The village is mentioned in the Doomesday Book — the great survey of England compiled for William the Conqueror between 1080 and 1086.

The Church of the Blessed Virgin Mary appears to have been built around 1120-30 and enlarged in the decade from 1170. It is rightly described as "Norman".

The porch has a Crucifix, and a sundial date 17 with the words "Certa ration" which, freely translated, means "The right time."

Kilburn in days of Yore

The south doorway is typical Norman work with two rows of chevron and a billet hood. The tower was built in stone in 1667. A fine iron chest, made in Kilburn in 1854, contains the registers dating from 1575 (the universal keeping of parish registers was ordered in 1538); church wardens' accounts from 1759 to 1900; the Inclosure Award (1829); the Tithe Award (1847), and many other interesting parish records.

The north aisle dates from the time the church was extended around 1170 — the line of the earlier north wall being marked by the fine pillars which are 6ft in circumference.

The Chapel of St Thomas was doubtless in honour of Thomas Becket, the Archbishop of Canterbury who was murdered in his cathedral in 1170 and who became a popular Saint.

Kilburn in 1907

The little chapel was refurnished in 1958 as a memorial to Robert Thompson, the Kilburn craftsman whose oak furniture, signed with a mouse, has made the village famous around the world.

A Brass in the floor commemorates a curate who died in 1721/2. Nearby are two fine grave slabs attributed to the late 13th century. The one with a pastoral staff was probably made for an Abbot of Byland, or a Prior of Newburgh.

The other, a very rare type, shows the shield with a round boss and the long-shafted "Martel", or fighting hammer of a "champion."

Kilburn Parish Church

33

An ecclesiastic was not supposed to shed blood, so he employed a champion to take his place in "trial by combat" — a Norman method of settling a case in dispute.

It is believed that Kilburn's champion fought for the Abbot, or Prior.

The Norman Chancel Arch has two orders of chevron, and a billet hood; a medieval window remains by the Priest's Door in the south wall while the three bells in the tower — and the east window of 1880 — were installed in memory of the first vicar, George Richardson, who was in charge from 1868 to 1879.

Robert Thompson was a legend in his own lifetime, and the pews in the Nave were made by his craftsmen and given to the church in 1970/71.

A drawing of Kilburn Village School by the late YEP artist, Thack.

Another Thack drawing - the foot of the Hambleton Hills

Jokers wild!
Did you know...?

OVER the decades, Kilburn's prominent and eye-catching White Horse has fallen prey to practical jokers.

It's assumed to be a white mare. A favourite ploy over the years has been to change the mare into a stallion. In days of yore, the favoured way was to use builders' lime. But that was before the advent of plastic sheeting.

The White Horse has even been turned into a Zebra by people using strips of black plastic.

That same black plastic has also been used to create a saddle, a nose band and even a black eye.

A walk around the White Horse and Gormire Lake
By Yorkshire Evening Post Journalist Frank Wilkinson

THIS is a magnificent five mile ridge walk along the edge of the Hambleton Hills and offers some of the finest views in England.

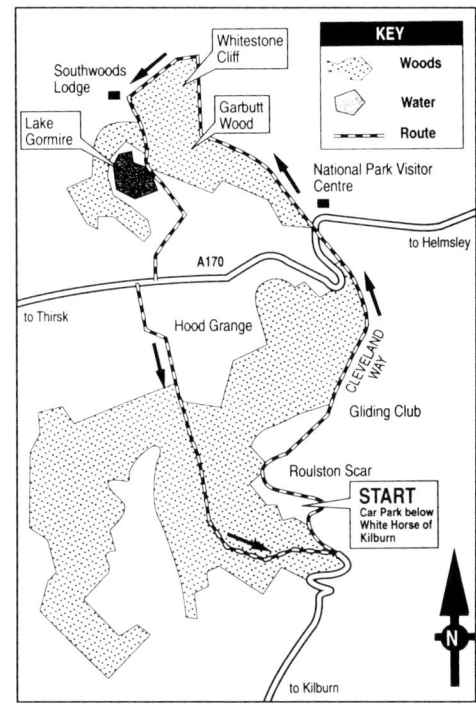

But country lovers can have a "double" up. There's a well-signposted alternative of one mile called the White Horse Walk.

The main walk starts from the car park directly beneath the White Horse of Kilburn.

35

Take the concrete path and steps up the right-hand side of the White Horse. At the top turn left and follow the Cleveland Way along the escarpment all the way to the top of Sutton Bank. The views are quite extraordinary across the broad Plain of York and, to the north, over the Vale of Mowbray to the Wensleydale fells.

As you pass the Yorkshire Gliding Club (keep your head down!), watch out for a footpath, the Thief's Highway, cutting back down to the left through Roulston Scar.

Short Walk

This is the way to go if you are doing the short walk, returning to the car park by well-marked forestry tracks.

The Thief's Highway was an escape route for highwaymen who preyed upon travellers on the Hambleton Drove Road. It is said the Scots used this path to surprise the English forces under the unfortunate King Edward II at the Battle of Byland which was fought nearby at Oldstead in 1322.

Edward had just returned from a punitive raid over the Scottish border but the Scots — still riding high in the aftermath of Bannockburn eight years earlier — chased him and caught his troops unawares.

Routed

The English were routed and Edward fled to the safety of the city walls of York.

As you approach Sutton Bank, Gormire Lake can be seen nestling in the trees down on your left. The path along the escarpment ends at a viewpoint with a telescope.

Sutton Bank has, arguably, the best view in the whole of England. On a clear day, it is claimed, you

An Autumn scene

can watch a train leave York Station and follow it all the way to Darlington.

Castle

An indicator stone points out Knaresborough Castle (19 miles), York (20 miles), Richmond (24 miles) and Great Whernside (32 miles).

Before crossing the Sutton Bank road to continue along the escarpment, break your journey and call at the National Park visitor centre. There is a tearoom and toilets.

Return to the top of Sutton Bank and turn right along the obvious path (signposted Cleveland Way and Sneck Yate).

The path continues to offer superb views as it approaches the 70ft Whitestone Cliff.

Whitestone Cliff has a more romantic alternative name — White Mare Crag — derived from one of the countless legends associated with this area.

Knight

The story is that an unfortunate knight, one Henry de Scriven, who had a black Barbary stallion, coveted the white Arab mare belonging to the Abbot of Rievaulx. One pitch-black night, by trickery, Henry persuaded the Abbot to swap horses for a wild gallop.

What poor Henry didn't know was that the Abbot was the Devil in disguise.

The white mare carried Henry straight over the cliff to his doom.

As he went over the edge, he looked around to see the Abbot swooping above him with cloven feet and horns.

Beyond Whitestone Cliff, the path dips slightly and bears right to follow the rim.

After a couple of hundred yards, at a signpost, cut back sharply left down the hill to enter Garbutt Wood nature reserve.

The track, often muddy, leads to a junction. Go right at the bridleway sign and continue on this main track all the way to near the bottom of the wood where another path comes in from the left.

Two Tracks

The meeting of these two tracks forms a definite "V". If you emerge from the wood, you have gone too far and should retrace your steps. Turn left at the "V" junction, over the duck boards to Gormire Lake, taking care not to tread on the frogs.

Gormire Lake is the perfect spot for lunch.

With Semerwater and Malham Tarn, it is one of only three natural lakes in Yorkshire.

It is something of a geological freak, having been formed 10,000 years ago when it was cut off and left behind by a glacial landslip.

It has no feeder or outlet, seemingly regulating itself by underground drainage.

One theory is that an underground stream flows out towards Kirkbymoorside and this is supported by an old story about a goose with more courage than discretion.

Goose

According to the tale the goose penetrated this secret tract of water and emerged, alive but minus feathers, 12 miles away in Kirkbymoorside.

The shoreline path leads out through a gate into a green lane and Gormire Farm. The next section is tricky and it is easier to walk straight down to the road and turn right.

However, if you want to follow the public right of way, turn right and left between the farm buildings to a metal gate.

At the fork just ahead, go left to another metal gate which guards a crop field.

A glance at the 1:25 000 map shows the right of way goes diagonally right across the field to the far corner. But there is no path over the ground, and no exit when you get to the field corner. So don't bother.

Instead, after climbing over the gate, take the slightly-discernible path going almost straight across the field, obviously preferred by the farmer.

Turn right along the hedge, then left through a gap and then right again to walk along with the hedge on your right.

When the hedge finishes — the public right of way should emerge at this corner — turn half left down the hill aiming for the obvious gateway in the bottom right-hand corner of the field.

Turn right along the road for 200 yards to a footpath sign on the left. Cross the stile and go across the field, past a long wooden post, to Hood Grange. On crossing the stile, turn right for a few paces and then go left through the gate (signposted Hood Hill).

Footbridge

Now over the footbridge and turn left through the gate along the fence. This fine field path curves right to enter Hood Hill plantation by a single-file track.

At the broad forestry road, turn left with Roulston Scar dominating the skyline. Stick with the main track all the way (about a mile) until it climbs uphill to meet another broad track. Turn right here. The broad track leads out into the metalled road up White Horse Hill. Turn left for the final, steep, pull to the car park. You've made it!

• Frank Wilkinson's popular Walking with Wilkinson column moved from its Friday slot to Wednesdays from April 24, 1995, in the *Yorkshire Evening Post*.

How far can you see?

An alternative view from the horse.

THOMAS Goodrick, in his verses, drew attention to the view thus: "To gaze across the landscape, so beautiful and grand,

"O'er the golden Vale of Mowbray, one of the finest in the land!"

Thomas could well have added The North York Moors, the Vale of Pickering, the Yorkshire Wolds, the Howardian Hills and the Vale of York.

Beyond the Vale of Mowbray, which is the name given to that part of the Vale which lies to the West of the North York Moors, can be seen Wensleydale, Swaledale and Nidderdale, and the hills beyond which border Cumbria and Lancashire.

With the help of binoculars, and given exceptionally clear conditions, the hills above Wharfedale and Airedale can be seen. So can the higher northern suburbs of Leeds. All this and the back drop of the Pennines with Pen-y-Ghent and Whernside standing out in stark relief.

Pen-y-Ghent

Immediately below the escarpment lies the wide valley of the Coxwold-Gilling Gap. This is a geological fault which joins the Vale of Mowbray to the Vale of Pickering and an intricate system of inter-connecting valleys caused by actions of ice and melt-water on the collapsed Jurrasic rocks on the north side of the fault.

Panoramic

Casting the eye round from east to west reveals a fascinating panoramic view of the history of this part of Yorkshire from the ancient to the modern and back again.

To the east, on the hill top, is Scots Corner — not Scotch Corner (which is near Richmond). Frank Wilkinson describes the battle that took place here in his walk on previous pages.

A little further to the east, and still on the hill top, a slim stone tower can be seen through the trees.

It's Oldstead Observatory, erected by local people to commemorate the Coronation of Queen Victoria in 1837.

Carved

A carved stone plaque, and an appropriate set of verses, can be found above the entrance. Below, hidden in the valley, is the village of Oldstead where the Byland Monks lived for 30 years before they moved to Byland Abbey.

Still to the east there are the ruins of the Cistercian Abbey at Byland. In the 12th and 13th centuries Byland was the headquarters of a large farming and business empire which took in a large part of the adjacent land and vast acreages further afield.

Valley

The surrounding valley contains the archaeological remnants of the Monks' fish ponds, dye works, bleach ponds and mill races.

Of the farmsteads strung across the valley, no less than eight have the name "Grange".

This indicates that they were once farms owned and worked by the monks. The Abbey Church, almost as big as Westminster Abbey, is an indication of their commercial success and prosperity.

Immediately behind, and about four miles further east, lies the Castle at Gilling — home of the Fairfax family, famous for their role in the Civil War in the 17th century.

Priory

Looking towards the middle distance, and to the south, lies the stately home — Newburgh Priory.

Its large fish pond often reflects the midday sun back to the White Horse. This is the site of an Augustinian Priory which was contemporary with Byland.

The Augustinian canons never achieved the prosperity of their Cistercian neighbours and concentrated on pastoral and evangelical work, providing priests for the surrounding churches in return for gifts of land and money from the large landowners.

Little remains of the original Priory because it was turned into a country seat for the Belassis family in the 16th and 17th centuries.

The Belassis's supported the King in the Civil War which put them on the opposite side to their neighbours, the Fairfax dynasty.

About three miles beyond Newburgh, Crayke Castle can be seen prominent on the hill above the village.

Minster

Beyond, in the misty distance, are the towers of York Minster — often looking dark in the middle of the day, but standing out white in the rays of the early morning or late evening sun.

Beyond York, and slightly to the south, a semi-circle of modern structures intervene; the power station cooling towers at Drax. Eggborough and Ferrybridge are slightly to the west. And further away still, the hills of north Leeds and Bradford are visible.

York Minster

Now look south west, and in the middle of the vale — below a conical hill near Boroughbridge — lies the remains of the old Roman town of Aldborough. Behind it, the tall spire of Knaresborough Parish Church leads the eye across to Harrogate.

In the middle of the Vale of Mowbray, the tower of the impressive church in the market town of Thirsk stands out.

Thirsk was the seat of the Mowbray family in the 12th and 13th centuries. At the time they owned the bulk of the land immediately surrounding the Hambleton Hills. Their castle at Thirsk is long gone.

A short walk westwards from the top of the horse brings you to the top of the cliff known as Roulston Scar. The area below is for reasons unknown, called "Happy Valley".

The old Monastic Grange of Hood can be seen. It's now a farm house, but it was the first dwelling house for the small party of monks who were eventually to found Byland Abbey.

Ice Age

West of "Happy Valley" is Hood Hill, an example of the effect of Ice Age erosion.

The crag and tail shape is due to the action of the glacier pressing down from the north creating a steep eroded north face and a long tail of deposited glacian debris stretching to the south.

It was on top of this hill that the Mowbrays built a "Motte and Bailley" Castle in the 12th century.

The wooden structure has long since disappeared, but the Mottes - or defensive trenches - can still be seen silhouetted against the sky.

The castle was built on this spot to protect the villages and religious settlements from bands of thieves who roamed this countryside stealing livestock from the Granges and game from the King's hunting park at Kilburn.

Soldiers

A book — the History of the North Riding — reveals that in the reign of Henry II, 300 soldiers were dispatched by the King to "put down the banditti which infest these mountains."

The robbers were confronted on Hood Hill, and defeated. The gap between Roulston Scar and Hood Hill is known as the Devil's Leap.

Legend has it that the Devil, pursued by the forces of good, jumped from the Scar on to the Hill leaving a footprint on a large stone.

There was, indeed, a large rectangular stone weighing 20 tons or more perched on the top most summit of Hood Hill. On top of it was an impression very like a large footprint.

Low Flying

In 1953, however, the stone was hit by a low flying aircraft. Both the aeroplane, and the stone, completely disintegrated.

A legend also tells that the stone was a cairn alter of the Druids. In the 1940s, the hill top was the site of a firing range. Gun turrets from bomber aircraft were mounted there and the Royal Air Force gunners trained, firing across Happy Valley.

Grassy Bank

There's a grassy bank about 200 yards north of Roulston Scar and it's known as "Knowlson's Drop".

The story goes that Knowlson was returning home from a visit to the Hambleton Inn when he drove his horse and trap too close to the edge of the cliff. He is supposed to have slipped over the 200ft drop... and both he and the horse survived. Only the trap was beyond repair.

The RAF "frame" the White Horse

Robert Thompson and that mouse.

THE mouse "signature" of master wood carver Robert Thompson is known across the country, and around the world.

That Robert Thompson ever became a wood carver at all is down to his dogged determination — but fate had a hand in steering him towards his goal.

Born in the Old Hall, Kilburn, he was the son of the village joiner, carpenter and wheelwright.

But young Robert didn't begin his working life with his father in the joiner's shop. He was sent 60 miles away to the West Riding and apprenticed to a firm of engineers in Cleckheaton.

Serenity

He left the serenity of Kilburn and found himself among the hustle and bustle of this developing textile town.

Cleckheaton is famed for its "shoddy" — but as the teenage Thompson served his apprenticeship he vowed his work would never merit such a description.

Craftsman Mike Varley in Thompson Museum, Kilburn.

Life in the mill town soon took its toll. He hated the place, and by the time he was 20 wanted to get out of Cleckheaton, and quit mechanical engineering.

Robert yearned to be back home among the rolling acres around his beloved Kilburn — a place he only ever saw at weekends while he was apprenticed.

He asked his father if he could return — a request that was granted.

So it was a life in the village carpenter's shop for Robert from then on. He got all the rough jobs — mending farmers' carts, making gates and tackling numerous household repairs around Kilburn.

Carver

But he still wanted to be a master carver — an idea he'd got while on his journeys between Kilburn and Cleckheaton.

Robert travelled through Ripon and he kept stopping off and marvelling at the craftsmanship of that medieval master carver, William Bromflet.

The impressionable Thompson was captivated by Bromflet's work in the cathedral and said it was his dream to bring back to life the spirit of medieval oak work which had been dead for so many years.

He delved into library books and studied the properties and possibilities of oak.

Ripon Cathedral; Autumn Leaves

Robert soon discovered that English oak —quercus robur— was by far the best wood for the carver because it had a close grain and was exceptionally hard.

He also investigated what tools he would need to fashion and mould the oak.

Oak

Robert was completely immersed in the study of oak, and the tools he'd need if his dream was to come true.

He acquired some tools and started carving in his spare time. Soon he was a man who could build an ordinary looking bungalow near his village, and at the same time — around 1910 — make a pulpit for nearby Yearsley Church. The pulpit is believed to have been his first ecclesiological work.

His life was to change in May, 1919, when Sydney Mawe, who lived in the village, introduced Robert to Father Paul Nevill of nearby Ampleforth College.

Priest

Father Paul, the Catholic priest of Ampleforth, had told Mawe — the only Catholic living in Kilburn — that he was having difficulty finding a carpenter to make an oak cross big enough to carry a large figure of Christ for the crucifix he wanted to erect in Ampleforth cemetery.

Mawe had worked occasionally with Thompson and introduced him to Father Nevill. Thompson said he'd do the job.

He never looked back, orders from other churches started rolling in.

But there was still no mouse. That came when Robert and another carver, Charlie Barker, were carving a beam on a church roof.

Charlie is said to have murmured something about being poor as church mice.

On the spur of the moment, Robert carved one.

Mouse

Robert said later: "I thought how a mouse manages to scrape and chew away the hardest wood with its chisel-like teeth, and it works quietly; nobody takes much notice. I thought this was may be like this workshop hidden away in Kilburn village in the Hambleton Hills. It is what you might call industry in quiet places, so I put the mouse on all my work."

That tradition continues. Although Robert died in 1955, his business still thrives. It's run by his great grandsons — Ian, Peter and Giles Cartwright.

The Mouseman of Kilburn, like the White Horse, will never be forgotten!

Arthur Stone

Pioneers All!

By Arthur Stone, Chief Executive, Leeds and Holbeck Building Society.

THE White Horse of Kilburn is a landmark to the ingenuity, vision and foresight of two men — Thomas Taylor and John Hodgson.

Taylor's vision to have a hill figure of a horse carved on Roulston Scar became a reality after local schoolmaster, John Hodgson — aided by villagers — cleared the land. They were pioneers, and their horse was "born" in 1857.

Just 18 years later, in 1875, some other pioneers were at work in Holbeck, a suburb of Leeds.

They were the original founders of what today is the Leeds and Holbeck Building Society, and — like the visionary and the creator of the White Horse — they strove to do something for their community.

The pioneers of the Leeds and Holbeck Building Society served their community by promoting the virtue of thrift, and home ownership.

The industrial revolution changed the face of Holbeck. It had been described as a "pleasant village", quite detached from the town of Leeds, and approached through a large tract of meadowland.

As homes mushroomed, so workers attracted by mill jobs could be housed, the greenery disappeared.

With bad conditions, and low wages, the workers and their families faced real hardship.

Money

It was a desire to improve their lot that saw the establishment of building societies like the Leeds and Holbeck who would lend money to their members.

Helped by these loans, housing conditions did improve — but the environment around didn't. The air was polluted by factory chimneys belching out black, acrid, smoke.

The people wanted an escape route. The train proved the answer.

Leeds

Residents of inner city areas in places like Leeds found that a relatively short train ride would take them out in to the countryside where they could fill their lungs with crystal clear air and look at some stunning scenery.

I suspect the White Horse at Kilburn was a popular destination for many city dwellers eager to escape, even for just a few hours, the smelly atmosphere around their homes.

Early Visitors

I'm convinced that lots of our members would have been early visitors to Kilburn, and many may have picnicked on the cliff face.

I think the Leeds and Holbeck Building Society is in a class of its own, just like the White Horse of Kilburn.

The Society, which started from humble beginnings but now has branches nationwide, is proud to be the sole sponsor of this book — **Kilburn and Its Horse.**

Heritage

The hill figure is part of our Yorkshire heritage, part of our environment, and an attraction that's worth saving for future generations.

I hope you have enjoyed reading about the White Horse; about Robert "Mouseman" Thompson and may tackle one of Frank Wilkinson's walks.